Going Deeper: Learning more about the Christian faith

by nate kupish

First Edition: December 2019

ISBN: 9781792109447

For the young people a part of 26 West Church. May you continue learning to enjoy and follow Jesus well in your everyday moments.

I've known Nate Kupish for more than a decade now, both as a friend and fellow pastor at 26 West Church. Nate is a gifted strategist, leader, writer and more. I'm thrilled to recommend Going Deeper: Learning more about the *Christ*-ian faith because it comes from Nate's deepest desire; to help move people from talking about God to experiencing His transformative love. Read this book slowly. Relationship can't be hurried. Knowing God takes time. It's a pursuit that is always worth the investment. Read this book devotionally. The path is clear and content rich in wisdom. Yet the heart of the work and its author is to help us discover the One who made and knows and calls us by name. Thanks Nate, for your life, your words, and your care.

Jose Zayas
Pastor of Teaching & Leadership, 26 West Church
& Founder, Good News Today

Contents

Preface

If you want to learn more about the Christian faith, but going to Bible College or Seminary isn't going to happen anytime soon, then this book is for you.

Twelve easy to read chapters, each one unpacking an important theological understanding within the Christian faith. God, humanity, the Law, holiness & sin, the Gospel, big theological words that show God's love for us, baptism & communion, prayer, the Church, the new heavens and the new earth, our life work, and the Bible.

May we allow God's words to change and shape and lead the way we think in hope of seeing our heavenly Father, Jesus, and God's Spirit for who they really are. A good God who loves us, is for us, is with us, and wants us to know Him.

Here's the big idea of this book

Recently, I was at our eye doctor getting my vision tested. The Optometrist helping me casually said, "Let's use the *phoropter* for your *refraction*."

My eyes must have gotten really big because she quickly backpedaled saying, "Sorry, I mean… let's have you look through a few lenses to figure out your current prescription."

Yeah… okay, now *those* are words I understood.

You see, big words – though rich with meaning and helpful in explaining concepts quickly to those with an academic background – can create confusion and distance between people. I think this is especially true when it comes to reading the Bible and learning the way of Jesus in a culture that often avoids depth.

That said, I want to help you go deeper in discipleship to the person of Jesus by distilling Bible College and Seminary level content into everyday language you can wrestle with.

I put this book together to help you learn a basic systematic theology of the Christian faith using everyday language.

Systematic theology is the study of God using an ordered approach.

Some of the words and ideas we'll explore together include *justification, eschatology, sin, resurrection, communion, and soteriology.*

Don't worry, I promise it'll make more sense as we go. You'll even find that throughout this study, you'll watch videos produced by my friends at The Bible Project[1] (jointhebibleproject.com). I think you'll enjoy their seriously incredible work in making the Scriptures easier to understand. I can't say enough good things about them.

But let's be honest, at this point, even while on page two,

some of you may be wondering why this stuff matters? Why care about specific words, concepts, or ideas?

Good question. The reason this stuff matters is because having a basic understanding of these life-shaping truths can help us enjoy Jesus more in our everyday moments. And ultimately, I think that's our greatest challenge.

When we were kids, we only understood the basic and straightforward words our parents used. Food. Eat. Water. Dog. My little boy Ezra calls everything, "baba." And while I'm proud of him, I'm also excited for him to expand his vocabulary as he grows up. I think learning a bit about systematic theology is kinda like that for our faith.

I hope for you to grow in your understanding of the goodness of God through the study and practice of the Christian faith, and I hope this short book becomes one tool to help you along the way.

It's not uncommon for the Christian faith to digress into a club we join, a group we grow up in, or simply be some agreement of certain truths we say we believe. And while clubs help us feel a part of something, and groups allow us to share experiences with others, and agreeing to an ordered way of life can be helpful for both, none of these things change us on the inside. They're all external. Plus, when a club, group, or agreement is the starting point for faith, they'll most likely be the endpoint and focus too, which misses God's heart in any of this.

So what *is* the Christian faith then?

The Christian faith is an ongoing response to the God who is over us, loves us, is for us, with us, and wants us to know Him. It's a life centered around the *Christ* (more on that later) that shapes us to live like His family, marked by peace and joy[2]. It's a life outlined for us in the Scriptures, which means we don't have to be the ones trying to figure out what's good and right, hoping it leads to a full and whole life. Jesus invites you and me to believe what He believed and live the way He lived.

But when it comes to someone else telling us what's best, many people live believing everything is relative. "What's true for you is true for you and what's true for me is true for me."

This kind of statement floods the thinking our day. But to say truth doesn't exist is an attempt to establish truth, the exact opposite of what it claims. So, the question is not *if* truth exists, but *where* truth is found.

For Jesus people, truth is received primarily from the

voice of God known through history, written down in the Bible (or "Scriptures"). It's where we learn about God and people and culture and how the world works.

And while the Bible is a big book made up of sixty-six smaller books, it's the same story over and over. It's a story about a loving God who creates humanity to live full lives in harmony with Him, each other, and creation. But humanity rejects God's way and presence, only to experience the world then spirals down into chaos and brokenness. Even still, again and again, God is patient and kind[3], calling humanity **TO TURN AROUND AND RETURN TO HIM**.

There's an ongoing invitation, every second and minute and hour and day for people to return to closeness with God and to put our hope in a God-promise that He'll return, restore, and remake the world one day soon. And that in spaces all around us, it's happening now too.

The Bible gives us a window into the lives of people who wrestled with who they *thought* was good and right and powerful and able to restore the world. God or themselves? It's a historical account that stretches from before time and into today and tomorrow. It's the same story we find ourselves in, and the same God-invitation continues to you and me.

In some chapters, you'll read about different ways people interpret specific topics in the Bible. I want you to get familiar with the words and views. But remember, don't get caught up in the variants. Stick with the big idea, *that God is good, and we can trust Him.*

So this book is a tool for you to go deeper in your learning of life-shaping God-truths. God telling us what's real and right.

And as we learn, may we **ALLOW GOD'S WORDS TO CHANGE AND SHAPE AND LEAD THE WAY WE THINK** because it's in that process where we'll see our heavenly Father, Jesus, and God's Perfect Spirit for who they really are. A good God who is over us, loves us, is for us, with us, and wants us to know Him.

He's everything we long for. May you continue to learn to enjoy and follow Jesus well.

A big hug,
nate kupish

Don't skip this page

This book has three parts.

Part one explores the narrative of Scripture. What's this story we find ourselves in all about? The story of the Bible is one of hope and peace and resurrection. It's a story about Love healing everything that wants to be healed, and us being called by name to join in.

Part two is all about framing our faith. We'll look at twelve important understandings within the Christian faith. It should be noted that faith is relational, not just some system, concept, idea, or principle... more on that later.

Then in part three, we'll walk through a few helpful words, ideas, and themes. Let's call it, *"What's that mean?"*

As you read, you'll find some words that **LOOK LIKE THIS**. Simple definitions of these words can be found in *Part 3: What's that mean?*

Finally, I hope you take time to smile and talk with God as you go deeper in your learning about the **CHRISTIAN** faith. Please don't become a smart jerk who thinks they know everything about God :)

Part one: Exploring the narrative of Scripture. What's this story we find ourselves in all about?

The Scriptures are historical documents recording the thoughts, interactions, struggles, and celebrations of real people in real places with God, each other, and themselves. It includes a handful of writing styles and types of literature. From narrative to poetry to songs to letters to bite-sized wisdom takeaways, the **BIBLE** has it all. The Bible is full of metaphors and countless literary devices. It's a roadmap to where humanity has been, where we are today, and where we're headed. But it's even more than that it's where we learn what God is like and find an invitation to a free life. A full life. The life we're all longing for. The Bible calls it *eternal life*, and it started before we ever became aware.

It's all there.

Let's start by watching these five videos:

- **The Story of the Bible** (thebibleproject.com/explore/how-to-read-the-bible)
- **Plot In Biblical Narrative** (thebibleproject.com/explore/how-to-read-the-bible)
- **Exile:** (thebibleproject.com/explore/exile)
- **TaNaK / Old Testament** (thebibleproject.com/explore/tanak-old-testament)
- **New Testament Overview** (thebibleproject.com/explore/new-testament-overview)

Having watched these videos, and pulling from what you may already know, can you outline the story of the Scriptures?

See if you can play through the narrative in your mind, recognizing and being able to explain each part briefly. You may find it helpful to explore some of the Old and New Testament (book-specific) videos on The Bible Project to fill in missing pieces.

Here are a few key moments along the way.

The Genesis account

The fall of humanity

Abram & God's promise (Genesis 18)

Isaac

Jacob (Israel)

The twelve tribes

Egypt

Moses & Aaron

The Law

Joshua

Judges & Kings

David, Solomon, & the divided tribes

The exile

The message of the prophets

Jesus

The twelve disciples

Jesus' death, burial, & resurrection

The Holy Spirit is given

The church

The letters
(think *most of the New Testament
as it's being written*)

Jesus' return

The new heavens and the new earth

Having a big-picture understanding of the narrative of
Scripture, how would you summarize it in twelve words
or less?

Write it out here:

Part two: Framing our faith. Twelve important understandings within the Christian faith.

Here's the one's we'll work through:

1. God
2. Humanity
3. The Law
4. Holiness and sin
5. The Gospel
6. Big theological words that show God's love for us
7. Baptism & Communion
8. Prayer
9. The Church

10. The new heavens and the new earth
11. Our life work
12. The Bible

You'll find some chapters to be short and sweet, while others are longer. For those that are longer, you'll notice the longer stuff (called, "Going even deeper") is optional. But regardless of how in-depth each one is, every chapter follows this format:

- The big idea
- Verse to put to memory
- Going deeper
- Bible Project videos to watch
- What does this mean for me today?
- Something I learned in this chapter
- A question raised in this chapter

We could spend our entire lives studying and learning more about the Christian faith, God's way of thinking and living within the world, but that's not the goal here.

The goal is for you to learn, but for that information to lead to your transformation. To become more of the person God has created you to be as a disciple of Jesus. A person who loves God and people as you moment by moment practice putting your trust and enjoyment in the perfect love that is the Father, Jesus, and Holy Spirit, adopting the everyday faith of Jesus.

Faith comes by knowing the character of God, not by trying to have more faith. So ultimately, each chapter points us to the goodness of God.

It's that simple.

1. God

The big idea

God is the creator and sustainer of all things. And God is both knowable and good.

Verse to put to memory

"And he passed in front of Moses, proclaiming, "The Lord, the Lord, the compassionate and gracious God, slow to anger, abounding in love and faithfulness, maintaining love to thousands, and forgiving wickedness, rebellion and sin. Yet he does not leave the guilty unpunished; he punishes the children and their children for the sin of the parents to the third and fourth generation."

Exodus 34v6-7

Going deeper

Who or what is God?

God is the creator and sustainer of all things. And God is both knowable and good.

The Bible says, *"For those who are led by the Spirit of God are the children of God. The Spirit you received does not make you slaves, so that you live in fear again; rather, the Spirit you received brought about your adoption to sonship. And by him we cry, "Abba, Father." The Spirit himself testifies with our spirit that we are God's children.*[4]*"*

Did you catch all the relational words used?

Led. Children. Received. Make you. Brought about. Adoption. Sonship. We cry (meaning *we can cry out to*). Abba. Father. Testifies with. We are God's Children.

God is undoubtedly both knowable and good.

So when we think of God, we must start with what God has revealed to us about Himself.

Though the word *Trinity* is not a Bible word, it can be a helpful theological term that gives us a starting place in recognizing how God has chosen to reveal Himself to us. We'll explore the word *Trinity* a bit more in the following videos and *Going even deeper* sections of this chapter.

Bible Project videos to watch

- **God** (thebibleproject.com/explore/god)
- **YHWH / LORD** (thebibleproject.com/explore/shema-listen)
- **The Messiah** (thebibleproject.com/explore/the-messiah)
- **Holy Spirit** (thebibleproject.com/explore/holy-spirit)

What does this mean for me today?

For some of us, it's our day to receive God's grace for our broken ways of thinking and acting. It's our day to move from hearing and step into responding to God's invitation to come close. He's been speaking to you since you were young and has never left your side, you can talk to Him like you talk to a friend.

For others, it may be taking a chunk of time away from friends and phones to be still with God as you give your attention to His invitation-words to know Him more today.

Something I learned in this chapter

A question raised in this chapter

Going even deeper (totally optional, but suggested)

The Scriptures teach, and God has revealed Himself through Trinitarian Monotheism. That's a fancy way of saying God is one (or *mono*), but also three (Father, Son, and Holy Spirit).

We get the word, *Trinity*[5], from the Latin word *trinitas*, meaning three-ness. And while the word *trinity* isn't in the Bible, church **THEOLOGIANS**[6] began using it somewhere around 200-500AD, "...to express the truth of who God is as revealed in Scripture.[7]"

In Greek, the word *Perichoresis* was used to refer to the perfectly unified relationship (or *dance*) between the Father, the Son, and the Holy Spirit.

To actively participate in this *dance* is to live in unity. While to reject it is to invite chaos and disorder into our lives.

Knowing God as Trinity and recognizing the perfect

relationship and unity of the Father, Son, and Holy Spirit lays a Biblical foundation for understanding the pattern of life itself. A model for our inside and outside worlds. It's the framework for aligning our lives with God (Galatians 5v16-26).

So that's where we start. Recognizing God is perfect unity. While at the same time remembering that's only an idea, understanding, words. God is so much greater than we can comprehend.

I like the way a guy named Victor White puts it.

"So soon as we become satisfied with any picture or image of God, we are in danger of idolatry: of mistaking the comprehendible image for the reality, of losing the numinousness, the mystery, the transcendent majesty of God. So soon as, consciously or unconsciously, we suppose we have grasped God, he must elude us, for he is always beyond the furthermost advance we make in knowledge about him.[8]"

Similarly, it's been said, "O all-transcendent God (what other name describes you?) what words can sing your praises? No word at all denotes you. What mind can probe your secret? No mind at all can grasp you. Alone beyond the power of speech, all we can speak of springs from you; alone beyond the power of thought, all we can think of stems from you.[9]" *Early Christian Prayers*

While human logic fails to be capable of fully capturing or explaining the Trinity, we see God as Father, Son, and Holy Spirit in the Scriptures.

So the big idea of God as Trinity is that *God is one in essence and three in person*.

Here are a few clarifications about God as Trinity:

1. God is not three different gods. That's called *polytheism* or *tritheism*. Instead, the Father is God. The Son is God. The Holy Spirit is God. The Father is not the Son. The Father is not the Holy Spirit. The Son is not the Father. The Son is not the Holy Spirit. The Holy Spirit is not the Son. The Holy Spirit is not the Father.

2. *Trinity* does not mean one God with three personalities or roles. That's called *modalism*. It's not that God revealed Himself as one face or facet, then another, then another while only being "that one" in that moment.

3. *Trinity* does not mean "one of them" created the "other two" or "two" created the "other one." That's called *subordinationism* and says, "...the Father was really God in the full authentic sense. The Son and the Spirit were thought of as lesser 'deities,' created by God the Father to reign as subordinate 'gods' over

all other created things."[10].

4. *Trinity* does not mean God is one but portioned into three parts. That's called *compositionism*.

That said, let's look at a few examples of God as Trinity in the Bible. I've bolded the references to make it easier to see.

From the Old Testament:

1. "Then God said, "Let **us** make mankind in **our** image, in **our** likeness, so that they may rule over the fish in the sea and the birds in the sky, over the livestock and all the wild animals, and over all the creatures that move along the ground." Genesis 1v26

2. "I will proclaim the Lord's decree: He said to me, "**You** are **my son**; today **I** have become **your father**." Psalm 2v7

3. "For to us a child is born, to us a **son** is given, and the government will be on his shoulders. And he will be called **Wonderful Counselor, Mighty God, Everlasting Father, Prince of Peace.**" Isaiah 9v6

From the New Testament:

1. "The angel answered, "The **Holy Spirit** will come on you, and the power of the **Most High** will

overshadow you. So the **holy one to be born** will be called the **Son of God**." Luke 1v35

2. "As soon as **Jesus** was baptized, he went up out of the water. At that moment heaven was opened, and he saw the **Spirit of God** descending like a dove and alighting on him. And a **voice from heaven** said, "This is **my Son**, whom **I love**; with **him I am** well pleased." Matthew 3v16-17

3. "Believe **me** (Jesus) when I say that **I** am in the **Father** and the **Father** is in **me**; or at least believe on the evidence of the works themselves." John 14v11

4. "And **I** (Jesus) will ask the **Father**, and **he** will give you another **advocate** to help you and be with you forever – the **Spirit** of truth. The world cannot accept **him**, because it neither sees **him** nor knows **him**. But you know **him**, for **he** lives with you and will be in you." John 14v16-17

5. "Therefore go and make disciples of all nations, baptizing them in the name of the **Father** and of the **Son** and of the **Holy Spirit**, and teaching them to obey everything I have commanded you. And surely **I** am with you always, to the very end of the age." Matthew 28v19-20

6. "All God's people here send their greetings. May

the grace of the Lord **Jesus Christ**, and the **love of God,** and the **fellowship of the Holy Spirit** be with you all." 2 Corinthians 13v13-14

7. "There is one body and one **Spirit**, just as you were called to one hope when you were called; one **Lord**, one faith, one baptism; one **God and Father** of all, who is over all and through all and in all." Ephesians 4v4-6

8. "But you, dear friends, by building yourselves up in your most holy faith and praying in the **Holy Spirit**, keep yourselves in **God's** love as you wait for the mercy of our Lord **Jesus Christ** to bring you to eternal life." Jude v20-21

9. "But when the kindness and love of **God** our Savior appeared, **he** saved us, not because of righteous things we had done, but because of **his** mercy. **He** saved us through the washing of rebirth and renewal by the **Holy Spirit**, whom **he** poured out on us generously through **Jesus Christ** our Savior,..." Titus 3v4-6

Well, there you have it, a few examples of God as Trinity in the Bible. And while we're on the topic, I thought it might be helpful to bring up something important. While it's often believed that each person of the Trinity operates in specific roles[11], God, though three, is one *essence*. God is one living, unchanging, and relational being whose attributes remain the same between Father, Son, and Holy Spirit.

Which raises the questions, "What is God like in essence, character, and attribute? And how does God as Trinity affect the way we relate to God and each other in our everyday moments?"

Let's start with what He's shown us about Himself.

Revelation is the process of making known what would otherwise be unknown.

Divine revelation is the process[12] of *God making Himself*[13] *known to people*[14]. This, of course, is necessary for us to *know* God[15]. Without self-disclosure, personal relationship is impossible.[16] How can one know another without revealing who they are? Think, "knowing" a celebrity based on limited information they disclose of themselves on social media as compared to a husband and wife who spend their lives together. The difference is monumental.

And the best part? God's not quiet about telling us who He is and what He's like. We can *know* God because He's told and is telling us everything we need to know to be in relationship with Him.

Which is to say... the purpose of God showing

us what He's like is relationship. That's a profoundly life-shaping truth if you allow it to shape the way you read the Bible.

Now, there are two basic types of revelation within the study of theology. *General* and *special*.

1. *General revelation* is creation (Psalm 19v1) and conscience (Romans 2) declaring the glory of God as creator and humans as the created. Romans 1v19–20 says, *"since what may be known about God is plain to them, because God has made it plain to them. For since the creation of the world God's invisible qualities —his eternal power and divine nature—have been clearly seen, being understood from what has been made, so that people are without excuse."*

2. *Special revelation* is God making Himself known through[17] the Scriptures, Messiah Jesus (more on that title later), prophecy, the church, dreams, etc. which reveal God as redeemer (Psalm 19v14) and humanity needing to be redeemed[18]. Jesus said, *"All things have been committed to me by my Father. No one knows the Son except the Father, and no one knows the Father except the Son and those to whom the Son chooses to reveal him."*[19]

Okay, so God has revealed Himself to us, but what's He like? Is God an angry old *man* up in the sky just waiting to punish people? Or is He a tender, kind to everyone Jesus who carries a lamb in one arm and a baby in the other as His perfectly blow-dried hair flows freely in the wind?

Well, neither, but sadly some form of these two pictures aren't uncommon when thinking about God. So, let's look at what *is* true about God through the lens of essence, attribute, and character.

God is love (essence).
He showed loved (attribute).
Therefore God is loving (character).

And catch this, the Scriptures use the phrase, *"the God of Abraham, the God of Isaac, and the God of Jacob"*[20] at least fourteen times. In other words, God *"is the same yesterday and today and forever."*[21]

Therefore, what God revealed about Himself in the past is still true about Him today and will continue to be true about Him in the future. Come on, that's good news!

So what has God shown us about Himself? I bet you know where we'll look to find out.

Yup, the Bible.

One of the primary texts to see what God (Father, Son, and Holy Spirit) is like is found in Exodus 34v6-7. Here's what it says:

"And he passed in front of Moses, proclaiming, "The Lord, the Lord, the compassionate and gracious God, slow to anger, abounding in love and faithfulness, maintaining love to thousands, and forgiving wickedness, rebellion and sin. Yet he does not leave the guilty unpunished; he punishes the children and their children for the sin of the parents to the third and fourth generation."

From it, we see that God is:

- Compassionate
- Gracious
- Slow to anger
- Abounding in love and faithfulness
- Maintaining love to thousands
- Forgiving wickedness, rebellion and sin
- He does not leave the guilty unpunished

A brilliant teacher and friend of mine Gerry Breshears, offers a helpful list of Scriptures where we see stuff the Holy Spirit[22] does which gives us an even more full picture of what God is like:

- **Teaches and reminds:** Luke 12v12, John 14v26, 1 Corinthians 2v13
- **Bears witness:** John 15v26, 16v23

- **Guides, hears and speaks**: John 16v13
- **Glorifies Jesus and discloses Him**: John 16v14
- **Has a mind**: Romans 8v27
- **Knows, has a will**: 1 Corinthians 2v11
- **Loves**: Romans 15v30
- **Can be grieved**: Ephesians 4v30, Isaiah 63v10
- **Cries out**: Galatians 4v6
- **Leads and witnesses**: Romans 8v16
- **Shows**: Hebrews 9v8
- **Speaks**: Mark 13v11, Acts 1v16, 8v29, 10v19, 11v12, 13v2, 21v11; 1 Timothy 4v1, Hebrews 3v7, Revelation 2v7, 22v17
- **Can be sinned against**: Matthew 12v31
- **Can be lied to**: Acts 5v3
- **Can be insulted**: Hebrews 10v29
- **Encourages and comforts**: Acts 9v31

Are you getting the picture? God is both knowable and good!

We also see *proper names* used for God in the Scriptures, which like His characteristics, reveal more of His character:

- **God**: Hebrew for Elohim which means "Mighty One" (Genesis 1v1). Used 2606 times.
- **LORD**: Hebrew for YHWH or Yahweh which means "Creator and sustainer and pure being" (Exodus 6v3). Used 6519 times.
- **Lord**: Hebrew for Adonai which means "Ruler" (Genesis 15v2).

And *poetic descriptive names* used for God (mostly in the context of "Our...") that help us see even further what God is like:

From the Old Testament:

- **Light**: Psalm 27v1 (David is describing God's comfort, insight, and saving power in the midst of being attacked by his enemies.)
- **Fortress**: Psalm 91v2 (Again, in context of being saved from the attacker.)
- **Hiding place**: Psalm 32v7 (Again, in the context of being saved from the attacker.)
- **Cornerstone**: Psalm 118v22 (Not only a Messianic prophecy but also professing that God uses broken things to accomplish His plans and purposes.)
- **Redeemer**: Psalm 19v14 (David describes God as the One who forgives and restores him from his sin.)
- **Deliverer**: Psalm 144v2 (David is describing God as a firm place to stand, the One who trains Him, protects Him, and delvers Him when being attacked.)
- **King of Israel**: Zephaniah 3v15 (The prophet describes God as the perfect King who forgives His people and calls them His own again.)
- **The Most High**: Deuteronomy 32v8 (Moses, the author, describes God as the One who created all things and people.)
- **Shepherd**: Genesis 49v24 (Jacob, describing God for his son Joseph, refers to Him as the One who cared for, or "shepherded" him.)

- **Potter**: Isiah 64v8 (The writer is crying out that God is merciful, confessing that He's the Potter and humanity is the clay – who are we to fight God?)
- **Rock**: Habakkuk 1v12 (The prophet is describing God as his salvation while others are perishing.)

From the New Testament:

- **Life**: John 11v25 (Jesus is speaking to Mary about her dead brother Lazarus comforting her by saying *He is the resurrection and the life* that Mary thinks is reserved only for "the last days".)
- **Deliverer**: Romans 11v26
- **Lamb of God**: John 1v36 (A powerful symbol in the Hebrew culture and Scriptures of the sacrificial lamb for Israel.)
- **Chief Cornerstone**: Mark 12v10 (The religious leaders have rejected Jesus, the One who God's entire family is built upon.)
- **Servant**: Acts 4v27 (Peter and John had just been released from prison for preaching about Jesus, and upon telling their friends they praised God by referring to Jesus as God's servant.)

And *communicable attributes* of God, which mean how God relates with others, that help us see further what God is like.[23] Here's just a few:

- **Love**: "God is love, and we are able to love as well."
- **Knowledge**: "God has knowledge, and we are able to

have knowledge as well."

- **Mercy**: "God is merciful, and we are able to be merciful too."
- **Justice**: "God is just and we, too, are able to be just."
- **Grace**: God is gracious, we too can be gracious.
- **Faithful**: God is faithful, we too can be faithful.

And *incommunicable attributes* of God, which mean the attributes that are unique to God, that help us see further what God is like:

- **Eternity**[24]: "God has existed for all eternity, but we have not."
- **Unchangeableness**[25]: "God is unchanging in his being, perfections, purposes, and promises, yet God does act and feel emotions, and he acts and feels differently in response to different situations. This attribute of God is also called God's immutability. God does not change, but we do."
- **Independence**[26]: "God does not need us or the rest of creation for anything, yet we and the rest of creation can glorify him and bring him joy."
- **Omnipresence**: "God is not limited to time or space. God is everywhere present, but we are present only in one place at one time."

Having laid all that out, here are eight things we can take away from the actions and character of God, primary proper and poetic names of God, along with the communicable and incommunicable attributes of the

God as seen in the Scriptures[27]:

1. **God is good and cares for us deeply.** The Father
   loves the Son, who loves the Spirit. We can live
   knowing we're safe, secure, and loved by God. This
   can move us to live from a place of seeking to love
   God in return.

2. **God is over us, for us, with us, and in us.** Here's a
   prayer I've found helpful, maybe you will too. *"God
   for us, we call You Father. God alongside us, we call
   You Jesus. God within us, we call You Holy Spirit. You
   are the Eternal Mystery that enables, enfolds, and
   enlivens all things, even us, and even me. Every name
   falls short of your goodness and greatness. We can
   only see who You are in what is. We ask for such
   perfect seeing as it was in the beginning, is now, and
   ever shall be. Amen."*[28]

3. **God is knowable.** The Son prays to the Father (in the
   garden), the Father speaks to the son (at His
   baptism), the Spirit leads people (like the Ethiopian
   Eunuch, through Phillip, in Acts 8) to Jesus. We get to
   live our lives directed towards getting to know and
   enjoy God.

4. **God has been, and always will be, actively involved
   in our lives** (or better put, that we're active in God's
   life.) God is eternal, or forever. We can live growing in
   presence awareness and invitation for God to change

us into the people He's created us to be.

5. **God is calling us to follow Him in our day to day moments.** The Trinity is pure unity, never pulling away from each other. We can live remembering that God's commands are always for the best, never seeking to destroy us but to mature us.

6. **God calls everything *spiritual*, that all of life matters.** Unlike Deism, God creates a physical universe and stays actively involved, mixing Spirit and material. We can live aware that all moments are God-moments. I can't emphasize this one enough :)

7. **God has given us everything we need to align our lives with His. He deserves our life and worship – our everything.** The Father withheld nothing from the Son (John 3v35), and the Spirit was given to us as a gift by the Son (2 Peter 1v3). We can live knowing that everything God asks of us is possible because He's already given us what we need to accomplish it.

8. But maybe most importantly, we see that God as Trinity reveals that His attributes are not based on emotion, as in: "God feels like showing mercy..." Instead, they flow from His essence, from who He is.

What God is like towards us reveals who God is.

And because everything is relational (the moon is not the moon without the earth), we see creation flowing from who God is... perfect relationship (Trinity). We see the brokenness of the world, recognizing our sin is the cause, and cry out for God's restoration. And we're invited to be *in Christ*[29], perfect relationship. We can live recognizing that we long for peace in all things because it's a reflection of God's own self.

2. Humanity

The big idea

God created people to enjoy Him, each other, and creation. **GLORIFYING** Him in the way they think and live.

Verse to put to memory

"Then God said, "Let us make mankind in our image, in our likeness, so that they may rule over the fish in the sea and the birds in the sky, over the livestock and all the wild animals, and over all the creatures that move along the ground." So God created mankind in his own image, in the image of God he created them; male and female he created them. God blessed them and said to them, "Be fruitful and increase in number; fill the earth and subdue

it. Rule over the fish in the sea and the birds in the sky and over every living creature that moves on the ground."

Genesis 1v26-28

Going deeper

God created male and female to enjoy Him, each other, and creation. Glorifying their creator in the way they think and live. But as we'll learn in Chapter 4, people rejected (and often still refuses to receive) God's **BLESSING,** which resulted in cosmic relational separation and brokenness between God, humanity, and everything around us. But God has not forgotten or dismissed us; instead, He came to us in the person of Jesus making a way for us to again be close with Him.

God fights to be with us. And as Jesus people, we've been promised that. Hebrews 13v5 quotes Joshua 1v5, *"I will never leave you or forsake you."*

Never means never. Nothing can separate us from the love of God.

Humanity enjoying God is relational, involving constant back and forth exchanges. When we have a proper picture of who God is, we can't help but listen and obey. It's when our thinking and understanding of Him becomes twisted and bent that we leave our purpose of enjoying Him, each other, and creation for something we think is better, but never is. We'll look more at what that "leaving" looks like in Chapter 4.

Bible Project video to watch

- **Image of God** (thebibleproject.com/explore/image-god)

What does this mean for me today?

One of the saddest and most destructive stories we hear every day about our identity is, "go find yourself... try everything to see what makes you feel happy."

It's a lie that leads to emptiness. A story which promises us provision in the form of greed, healing in the way of rejection or running away, peace in the form of momentary quiet, joy in the form of temporary entertainment, holiness in the form of moralism, and being on "God's good side" in the form of religion.

This story plays all around us, but it's not the best story. Thankfully the story God tells us is different. Very different.

God created us, and like any good parent, loves us too much to let us destroy our lives because of a lack of guidance. So instead of "go find yourself..." God tells us who He is, which in turn tells us who we are.

Here's an example. God says He's our healer. So, as His beloved, we're dependent on Him to heal us.

God's story is rich with identity and meaning, and purpose. It's no wonder one of the metaphors used in the Scriptures of God is *water in a dry land.*

Having been created by God on purpose, your life has meaning and purpose, and you'll grow in understanding and experiencing that purpose as you learn to enjoy God in your everyday moments.

"When we sin and mess up our lives, we find that God doesn't go off and leave us – he enters into our trouble and saves us. That is good, an instance of what the Bible calls gospel."[30] Eugene Peterson

Today, take a few minutes to be still. Set anything aside that calls for your attention. Read the following three verses, then ask God this question, "Tell me what you're like and show me who I am."

"So God created mankind in his own image, in the image of God he created them; male and female he created them." Genesis 1v27

"For I know the plans I have for you," declares the Lord, "plans to prosper you and not to harm you, plans to give you hope and a future. Then you will call on me and come and pray to me, and I will listen to you. You will seek me

and find me when you seek me with all your heart. I will be found by you," declares the Lord..." Jeremiah 29v11-14a

"For we are God's handiwork, created in Christ Jesus to do good works, which God prepared in advance for us to do." Ephesians 2v10

Something I learned in this chapter

A question raised in this chapter

3. The Law

The big idea

God is good and tells people the best way to live –
moment by moment, trusting Him. The evidence of trust
is obedience.

Verse to put to memory

*"Teacher, which is the greatest commandment in the
Law?" Jesus replied: "'Love the Lord your God with all
your heart and with all your soul and with all your mind.'
This is the first and greatest commandment. And the
second is like it: 'Love your neighbor as yourself.' All the
Law and the Prophets hang on these two
commandments."* Matthew 22v37-40

<u>Going deeper</u>

In Exodus 20, God gives a man named Moses (Israel's leader) Ten Words or commands on what it looks like to live His way. It was the way humanity was always created to live, which would, in turn, cultivate a full and whole life. God's family (Israel) was to think and act differently than the nations around them who were living in ways contrary to God's best.

God, like any good parent, gave these commands not only for rules sake but for His family to get to learn to trust and obey Him for their benefit too. God knew as they followed, they'd get to enjoy Him.

Remember, God is good and was inviting them to learn to trust Him in their everyday moments. That's why each of the commands, or words, had to do with everyday stuff. What they thought about, how they spoke, days of the week, relationships, stealing, lies, etc.

Among other reasons, here's two reasons the Ten Words were a gift rather than a burden. Even if it seemed the other way around at times:

1. It's easy to forget God is good, leaving His way for another. Our own. In the *Ten Words*, we see God is patient and kind, slow to anger, and abounding in love just like we learned about in Chapter 1.

2. God knows how life works better than we do and wants the best for us. He's so intent on us living a full life (or as both the writer of Psalm 1 and Jesus in Matthew 5 use the word "**BLESSED**" life) that He's clear about the repercussions of what happens when we refuse His law, His way, and His wisdom.

Let's look at an overview of the Law in Exodus 20v1-17[31]:

Commands 1-4 are about our relationship *with God*.

1. "No other gods, only Me." v3
2. "No carved gods of any size, shape, or form of anything whatever, whether of things that fly or walk or swim. Don't bow down to them and don't serve them because I am God..."v4-5a
3. "No using the name of God, your God, in curses or silly banter; God won't put up with the irreverent use of his name." v7
4. "Observe the Sabbath day, to keep it holy. Work six days and do everything you need to do. But the seventh day is a Sabbath to God, your God. Don't do any work..." v8

Commands 5-10 are about our relationship *with those around us*.

5. "Honor your father and mother..." v12a
6. "No murder." v13
7. "No adultery." v14

8. "No stealing." v15
9. "No lies about your neighbor." v16
10. "No lusting after your neighbor's house—or wife or servant or maid or ox or donkey. Don't set your heart on anything that is your neighbor's." v17

Seem simple enough right? Well, unfortunately, no one kept the Law perfectly (more on this in the next chapter) which only highlighted the fact that humanity wasn't perfect, not even close.

If the Law acted as a test, then our failure to keep it identified our need for saving if we ever wanted to be in right relationship with a perfect God. Romans 3v20 says it this way, *"Therefore no one will be declared righteous in God's sight by the works of the law; rather, through the law we become conscious of our sin."*

Later in the Biblical narrative, Jesus is asked a question about the Law and quotes **THE GREAT SHEMA** from Deuteronomy 6v4-9, a summary of *the Ten Words* God gave His people in Exodus (the intended fabric of relationships).

Picking up the story in Matthew 22v37-40, *"Teacher, which is the greatest commandment in the Law?" Jesus replied: "'Love the Lord your God with all your heart and with all your soul and with all your mind.' This is the first and greatest commandment. And the second is like it: 'Love your neighbor as yourself.' All the Law and the*

Prophets hang on these two commandments."

So, the Law was intended to be an expression and outworking and hands-on guide to loving God and loving people. It was for the good of humanity.

In Matthew 5, we learn that Jesus came to fulfill the Law. He did what no other person ever could, keeping the commands perfectly. In doing so, Jesus invites us to live not by rules any longer, but in relationship with Him.

Bible Project videos to watch

- **The Law** (thebibleproject.com/explore/the-law)
- **The Shema Series** (thebibleproject.com/explore/shema-listen)
  - Shema / Listen
  - YHWH / LORD
  - Ahavah / Love
  - Lev / Heart
  - Nephesh / Soul
  - Meod / Strength
- **The Covenants** (thebibleproject.com/explore/covenants)

What does this mean for me today?

We recognize there's *a best way* to live – being in an

ongoing relationship with Jesus. In this relationship we're led, taught, loved, disciplined, and encouraged. Today, every decision you make is an important one as God longs for you to know His love and care for you.

Find a rubber band (or something you can wear on your wrist) and let it be a reminder to you today of God's closeness and desire for you to talk with Him about everything.

Let Him shape you into who He says you're created to be as you agree with His way to live over your moods, feelings, or desires. And when He speaks, challenging your way, correcting or convicting you, listen and obey.

After all, not only is His way best, but He's God, and we're not.

Something I learned in this chapter

A question raised in this chapter

4. Holiness & Sin

The big idea

God is holy. Perfect, totally good, and set apart.
Humanity is not, but thinks and acts like we are, we sin.

Verse to put to memory

*As it is written: "There is no one righteous, not even
one; there is no one who understands; there is no one
who seeks God. All have turned away, they have together
become worthless; there is no one who does good, not
even one."* Romans 3v10-12

*"There is no one holy like the Lord; there is no one besides
you; there is no Rock like our God."* 1 Samuel 2v2

Going deeper

Sin is a departure from God's standards of uprightness. It begins with saying *no* to God, violating what He says is good and right and true and just. It can be a *thought* (inside of us) or an *action* (outside of us). Holiness, on the other hand, means unique or set apart. God alone is holy, but through Jesus, we can be forgiven, brought near to God and are made clean, right (or the Bible word is *righteous*), and holy.

The sin problem causes issues everywhere:

In relation to God, the Bible calls us enemies[32].

In relation to each other, we lie and cheat and steal and take advantage of and murder to get what we want.

In relation to the earth, we pollute and pillage.

In relation to ourselves, we seek identity and meaning and purpose in empty places.

In relation to food, we overeat and hoard rather than share.

And on and on.

Sin is nasty stuff, and we bear the full responsibility of it.

Holiness though has no error in it. It's perfect and good and right. In fact, anything not-holy or *unholy* cannot approach it. It'd be destroyed. This destruction is the issue of our sin and God's holiness. Without Jesus, we have no place in the presence of God. We'd die.

But holiness also makes one day a week special, a day for us to rest from working and doing and getting. See Genesis 2. And holiness makes regular everyday things special as God speaks to us through them. See Exodus 3.

Holiness and sin are a part of the same story, the story of a holy God saving humanity from the effects of sin.

Bible Project videos to watch

• **Holiness** (thebibleproject.com/explore/holiness)
• **Khata / Sin** (thebibleproject.com/videos/khata-sin)

What does this mean for me today?

Remembering God is holy (that there is no evil in Him whatsoever) can be a daily practice for us as God's family, even if taking only a few minutes to be still, giving our attention to Him. Being honest about our sin is essential. Recognizing God's grace is the reason we can, again and again, come close to Him.

Today, take a few moments to close your eyes and enter into Revelation 4 (below), a poetic description of God on

His throne. As you do, remember the cross. See your rebellion on Jesus as He takes it from you, making you clean, able to come before the throne of God!

"After this I looked, and there before me was a door standing open in heaven. And the voice I had first heard speaking to me like a trumpet said, "Come up here, and I will show you what must take place after this." At once I was in the Spirit, and there before me was a throne in heaven with someone sitting on it. And the one who sat there had the appearance of jasper and ruby. A rainbow that shone like an emerald encircled the throne. Surrounding the throne were twenty-four other thrones, and seated on them were twenty-four elders. They were dressed in white and had crowns of gold on their heads. From the throne came flashes of lightning, rumblings and peals of thunder. In front of the throne, seven lamps were blazing. These are the seven spirits of God. Also in front of the throne there was what looked like a sea of glass, clear as crystal.

In the center, around the throne, were four living creatures, and they were covered with eyes, in front and in back. The first living creature was like a lion, the second was like an ox, the third had a face like a man, the fourth was like a flying eagle. Each of the four living creatures had six wings and was covered with eyes all around, even under its wings. Day and night they never stop saying:

"'Holy, holy, holy is the Lord God Almighty, who was, and is, and is to come."

Whenever the living creatures give glory, honor and thanks to him who sits on the throne and who lives for ever and ever, the twenty-four elders fall down before him who sits on the throne and worship him who lives for ever and ever. They lay their crowns before the throne and say:

"You are worthy, our Lord and God,
    to receive glory and honor and power,
for you created all things,
    and by your will they were created
    and have their being."

Something I learned in this chapter

A question raised in this chapter

5. The Gospel

The big idea

The Gospel is good news. It's a message *and* a person (Jesus). It's the restoring heart of God made known through Jesus' life, death, and resurrection. And it results in a new life under the authority and care of the Spirit of God that includes *every part* of our lives – relationships, work, money, rest, and everything else.

Verse to put to memory

"For it is by grace you have been saved, through faith— and this is not from yourselves, it is the gift of God – not by works, so that no one can boast. For we are God's handiwork, created in Christ Jesus to do good works, which God prepared in advance for us to do."

Ephesians 2v8-10

Going deeper

The Gospel is both broad *and* specific. It's a message *and* a person (Jesus). It's the restoring heart of God made known through Jesus' life, death, and resurrection. And it results in a new life under the authority and care of the Spirit of God that includes *every part* of our lives – relationships, work, money, rest, and everything else.

Unwilling to step away from His turned stubborn-disobedient creation, God pursues the healing of all broken things so that they can function in fullness.

At the core of humanities brokenness is a separation from God. This separation is massive. In relationship to God, the Bible calls us enemies[33].

You've seen the issue in chapters 1-4, but now it's time to celebrate the solution!

Even in our brokenness, God comes after us, inviting us home. Always. Again and again.

And as we respond to His invitation, our lives change. We experience His with-ness, His presence. He speaks, showing us when we're heading in the wrong direction and teaches us what it looks like to turn around. What it looks like to align our lives with Him. Comforting us when we're discouraged. And everything else we need to live in our created intent.

Romans 5v6-11 puts it this way:

"You see, at just the right time, when we were still powerless, Christ died for the ungodly. Very rarely will anyone die for a righteous person, though for a good person someone might possibly dare to die. But God demonstrates his own love for us in this: While we were still sinners, Christ died for us.

Since we have now been justified by his blood, how much more shall we be saved from God's wrath through him! For if, while we were God's enemies, we were reconciled to him through the death of his Son, how much more, having been reconciled, shall we be saved through his life! Not only is this so, but we also boast in God through our Lord Jesus Christ, through whom we have now received reconciliation.

Bible Project videos to watch

- **Gospel** (thebibleproject.com/explore/gospel-word-study)
- **Euangelion / Gospel** (thebibleproject.com/explore/gospel-word-study)
- **Gospel of the Kingdom** (thebibleproject.com/explore/

gospel-kingdom)
- **The Messiah** (thebibleproject.com/explore/the-messiah)
- **Son of Man** (thebibleproject.com/explore/son-of-man)

What does this mean for me today?

The Gospel is good news. The good news that Jesus came to rescue sinners (that means everyone) and give us eternal life. Today, no matter where you're and what you've done, you have an invitation to trust Jesus (His death and resurrection) to forgive and transform you. This is a gift. A for-you gift. Jesus has already done everything to make this new life possible. But it's not automatic. We respond by turning to Jesus and trusting Him. If you've never received God's grace for your brokenness, today is the day. Talk to Him. He's already listening, excited to hear your voice.

If you have received God's grace for your brokenness, the invitation is the same. It's the story we find ourselves in and the air we breathe, the grace of God for us in all moments. He's everything we long for. Take a few minutes to do something (write, draw, sing, run, etc.) to celebrate His kindness.

Something I learned in this chapter

A question raised in this chapter

6. Big theological words that show God's love for us

The big idea

Let's look at some big theological words that show God's love for us. Ultimately they all point to the same thing; being a "good person" doesn't save us. God's grace saves us. This is the invitation each of these words offers.

Verse to put to memory

"... a person is not justified by the works of the law, but by faith in Jesus Christ. So we, too, have put our faith in Christ Jesus that we may be justified by faith in Christ and not by the works of the law, because by the works of the law no one will be justified." Galatians 2v16

"Once you were alienated from God and were enemies in your minds because of your evil behavior. But now he has reconciled you by Christ's physical body through death to present you holy in his sight, without blemish and free from accusation." Colossians 1v21-22

Going deeper

Language, both spoken and written, is a wonderful thing. Words allow us to move what's in our mind into someone else's. And what's even more amazing is how much a single word can hold.

Recently I was helping lead an event where we had a handful of photographers taking photos. After the event, each photographer sent me their images. But instead of sending me hundreds of files, they each sent me a single file. Just one. They had taken their many photos, dragged them into a folder, and zipped them. The name of that single .zip file was the name of the event. Without opening their file, I had a pretty good idea of what was inside... photos they'd taken during the event.

In a similar way, we often use one word to explain something that would otherwise take a long time to explain.

The word "zoo" helps communicate a place with tons of animals. Isn't it amazing that a three-letter word can bring so many images to your mind?

In **THEOLOGY**, we do the same thing. We use words to help capture big ideas.

This chapter is a basic overview of six big theological words within the Christian faith. Each is full of meaning. They are *atonement*, *salvation*, *reconciliation*, *justification*, *sanctification*, and *conversion*.

And while countless books have been written about each, our goal is to develop a basic understanding of these big theological terms that show God's love for us.

Let's start with *atonement*.

1. **Atonement** is the *full payment for a debt*. In the Christian story, Jesus' death paid for the death, or debt, that our sin causes.

The Bible project captures the meaning of atonement really well: "All over the New Testament, we hear how the death of Jesus was an atonement for our sins, covering the debt that humans owe God for contributing to all the evil and death in the world. The New Testament also talks about the atonement of Jesus Christ as a purification. Like the blood of the animal sacrifices, it is now Christ's blood that washes away all of the damage and side-effects of sin, purifying and sanctifying the world.[34]"

2. **Salvation** is God's rescuing work to save us from the effects of sin through Messiah (or, "The Christ") Jesus.

3. **Reconciliation** is making broken things whole. Jesus taking our place of deserved judgment is the ending of us being estranged from God.

4. **Justification** is God saying someone, like me and you, is not guilty (forgiveness), and even more is now **RIGHTEOUS** (acceptance).

It's external in that God speaks it over us, a one time moment. It's God's work for us, a new identity, by grace as we believe (faith).

5. **Sanctification** is the ongoing process of becoming more holy by the power of Holy Spirit in us.

It's internal in that our lives are being formed more into the people God says we are as we allow God's words to change and shape and lead the way we think, aligning our thinking and living with God's way.

It's the working out of our salvation because God is working in us by His power. And God's work for us by grace as we believe (faith).[35]

6. **Conversion** is the outcome of God-trust (faith) and repentance. It's trusting that God is truth, right, good, and that His way is the best way. This leads to a changing

of our minds about values. And a changing of gut about desires.

Bible Project videos to watch

- **Sacrifice & Atonement** (thebibleproject.com/explore/sacrifice-atonement)
- **The Messiah** (thebibleproject.com/explore/the-messiah)

What does this mean for me today?

When it comes to theology, it's easy to get caught up in the studying part. And while studying can absolutely bring glory to God, the truths we've been given are intended to lead us to God. Something to watch out for is an attitude of thinking we know more than others as we grow in knowledge. Today, as these words come to mind, try to see through them to the heart of what they mean for you and those around you.

Something I learned in this chapter

A question raised in this chapter

<u>Going even deeper (totally optional, but suggested)</u>

Sōtēria (σωτηρία) is the Greek word for "saved" and *logos* (λόγος) or *ology* being "the study of." Therefore, **soteriology** is the study of salvation.

Salvation means conversion, God's saving work, which began before the fall in Genesis 3 as God offered a covenant for humanity to "be saved" through Messiah Jesus[36].

Why did humanity need saving?

Ultimately, because of our relational rejection of God (not trusting God is who He says He is[37]), which leads to sin.

What can/is humanity be saved from?

- **Guilt** (what I've done) of past sin, now forgiven.
- **Shame** (what I am), given a new identity in Christ.
- The **power and authority of sin**, now under God's authority.
- **Alienation from God**[38] (resulting in condemnation), now children of God.

Salvation is past[39], present[40], and future[41]. Salvation is not a release into nothing, but into something. So what were/are/will we be saved into?

- **A full life** (Biblically defined as opposed to the world's values).

- **Ongoing relational interaction with God, each other, and creation.**

Salvation is God saving a community[42] for Himself, restoring righteousness and justice and integrity and health and value to function in shalom and peace with Himself, each other, and all of creation.

The enemy offers isolation and seeking answers for ourselves rather than trusting God. Salvation restores this damage.

We see God working for salvation and order in the chaotic history of time, or we can say at the *redemptive-historical level*. But we also see God working in individuals, or within a *personal-relational level*. In today's language, we may say "my testimony," or what God's doing in my life.

Just as an event can be described from multiple perspectives, *the process of salvation* can vary a bit based on theological systems[43]. That said, here's a few pieces that are agreed upon within Evangelical thought:

- Apart from God's grace, humanity is in and headed towards sin and death.
- Messiah Jesus' life, death, and resurrection is the only

solution to our sin and death.

- Justification and regeneration come by Messiah Jesus' grace alone through humanity receiving faith. We can't do anything to earn or cause it on our own.
- Salvation comes through hearing, and hearing comes through speaking (or sharing).
- The church's mission is **NON-DUALISTIC** worship, sharing the gospel, and building up the saints (God's people).
- We can know we're saved by Jesus.

Next question, who can be saved?

This is where the term *election* comes in. *Election* means "to choose." Ephesians 1v3 says God chooses humanity to be saved. The difference in perspective is *who makes the choice to be saved?*

- The Wesleyan-Arminian view says God looks into "the future" knowing who says "yes."
- A Calvinistic view says God chooses who He chooses.
- And an alternative says God's works in different ways with different people.

But regardless of your view of *election* based on the Scriptures, remember the big idea: *God is good, and we can trust Him.*

Salvation though, cannot exist without election and election without grace. So what is grace?

Grace is:

- God's unmerited favor[44] and unconditional acceptance.
- God's empowerment.[45]
- God giving life as He cleanses from sin.[46]

A profound example is Psalm 51v1, where David, having committed adultery and been called out by Nathan the prophet, cries out to God without anything to offer and pulls from Exodus 34v6-7 requesting that God show him mercy, unfailing love, and great compassion. David deserves death but comes before God with an understanding of the God of grace with the attitude that *I have no right to be here.*

Another example can be found in 2 Samuel 9v8. A man named Mephibosheth deserves death (because he's part of an old kingdom-line), but because David is king, and because his friend Johnathan has a son (Mephibosheth), he shows grace. We too, are a friend of Jesus (the Son), and the Father shows us grace because it's who He is.

I like how Gerry Breshears says it, "So what does the life of grace look like? Well, the life of grace looks to be like Mephibosheth and accept the call to sit at his table, to run the lands. Accepting His cleansing knowing we need it."

The person not willing to accept grace (when confronted with their sin) blame shifts, tries to explain their sin away, denies, spiritualizes, and offers religious practices to say, "look at what I'm bringing you! It's all good."

A life of entitlement says, "Well, I sin, but that's God's job to take care of." Whereas a life of grace never ignores sin. Living a life of grace always comes to Jesus for cleansing.

Grace is an offer which leads us into:

- **Conversion**[47] is the outcome of God-trust (faith) and repentance. It's trusting that God is truth, right, good, and that His way is the way. This leads to a changing of our minds about values. And a changing of gut about desires.
- **Justification**[48] is God saying someone, like me and you, is not guilty (being forgiven), but righteous (now accepted). It's external in that God speaks it over us, a one time moment. It's God's work for us, a new identity, by grace as we believe (faith)
- **Regeneration**[49] is God forming a new heart in us and the indwelling of His Spirit. It's a changing of our deepest desires.
- **Sanctification**[50] is the ongoing process of becoming more holy. It's internal in that our lives are being formed more into the one God says we are and continues each day as we devote ourselves to and live in purity. It's the working out of our salvation because

God is working in us by His power.

- **Glorification**[51] is the someday completion of salvation.

7. Baptism & Communion

The big idea

Baptism and communion are symbols and celebrations for the family of God.

Verses to put to memory

"Peter replied, "Repent and be baptized, every one of you, in the name of Jesus Christ for the forgiveness of your sins. And you will receive the gift of the Holy Spirit. The promise is for you and your children and for all who are far off—for all whom the Lord our God will call."

Romans 2v38-29

"And he took bread, gave thanks and broke it, and gave it

to them, saying, "This is my body given for you; do this in remembrance of me." In the same way, after the supper he took the cup, saying, "This cup is the new covenant in my blood, which is poured out for you." Luke 22v19-20

Going deeper

Symbols are everywhere.

When we see a red, white, and blue flag with fifty stars, we recognize the country it's pointing to. We see someone wearing a wedding ring and recognize the commitment they've made to another. Symbols are signposts pointing beyond themselves to something greater. In the same way, baptism and communion are super important and rich symbols in the Kingdom (or family) of God.

You may be familiar with both baptism and communion, but let's see what the Scriptures say about them. A good place to start and consistently return to.

Let's start with baptism:

After hearing the Gospel (check out how Peter presented it by reading Acts 2v14-37), people asked what they should do. Romans 2v38-39 records Peter's response. *"Peter replied, "Repent and be baptized, every one of you, in the name of Jesus Christ for the forgiveness of your sins. And you will receive the gift of the Holy Spirit. The promise is for you and your children and for all who are far off—for all whom the Lord our God will call."*

Then in Romans 6v3-4, we see why baptism is a one-time public act of going under the water and being brought back up. *"Or don't you know that all of us who were baptized into Christ Jesus were baptized into his death? We were therefore buried with him through baptism into death in order that, just as Christ was raised from the dead through the glory of the Father, we too may live a new life."*

Baptism is a linking of ourselves to Jesus by responding to his life (standing), death (being taken under the water), and resurrection (coming up from the water). And the best part? It leads to a new life. This is the celebration of what Jesus accomplished for us and our accepting His invitation into it!

Communion flows from baptism:

It's the ongoing remembering, **REPENTING**, and celebrating of Jesus' life, death, and resurrection. Jesus gave this active symbol of God-participation to His disciples. We see it in Luke 22v19-20: *"And he took bread, gave thanks and broke it, and gave it to them, saying, "This is my body given for you; do this in remembrance of me." In the same way, after the supper he took the cup, saying, "This cup is the new covenant in my blood, which is poured out for you."*

Here are a few more verses about communion to look up. I'd suggest reading a few lines above and below each verse to get a better idea of their context:

- 1 Corinthians 11v24-26
- Matthew 26v26-28
- 1 Corinthians 10v16-17
- John 6v53-54

Communion is something we get to do often with other Jesus people. What would it look like for you to invite others into taking communion with you during an upcoming meal?

Bible Project video to watch

- **Sacrifice & Atonement** (thebibleproject.com/explore/sacrifice-atonement)

Bible Project Podcast (optional)

- **Chaotic Waters & Baptism** (thebibleproject.com/podcast/design-patterns-bible-part-4-chaotic-waters-baptism)

What does this mean for me today?

For one, have I made the decision to be baptized yet? Why or why not?

Secondly, the next time you get to take the bread and cup (communion), how will what you've learned in this chapter change the way you think about it?

Find another Jesus follower today and celebrate communion!

Something I learned in this chapter

A question raised in this chapter

8. Prayer

The big idea

We were created for God's presence and ongoing 24/7 interaction. This back and forth was and is God's intention for the foundation of our lives. It's where we discover His heart and purposes and desires, and it's the place we're cared for by Him and given what we need to thrive in life. This is prayer.

Verse to put to memory

"And pray in the Spirit on all occasions with all kinds of prayers and requests. With this in mind, be alert and always keep on praying for all the Lord's people."

Ephesians 6v18

Going deeper

Like breathing, over time, prayer can become something we no longer think about, just do – our natural response to every moment.

We were created for God's presence and ongoing 24/7 interaction. This back and forth was and is God's intention for the foundation of our lives. It's where we discover His heart and purposes and desires, and it's the place we're cared for by Him and given what we need to thrive in life. This is prayer.

Jesus gives a walkthrough of the heart of prayer in Matthew 6v5-14.

Here's what He says:

"And when you pray, do not be like the hypocrites, for they love to pray standing in the synagogues and on the street corners to be seen by others. Truly I tell you, they have received their reward in full. But when you pray, go into your room, close the door and pray to your Father, who is unseen. Then your Father, who sees what is done in secret, will reward you. And when you pray, do not keep on babbling like pagans, for they think they will be heard because of their many words. Do not be like them, for your Father knows what you need before you ask him.

This, then, is how you should pray:

Our Father in heaven,
hallowed be your name,
your kingdom come,
your will be done,
on earth as it is in heaven.
Give us today our daily bread.
And forgive us our debts,
as we also have forgiven our debtors.
And lead us not into temptation,
but deliver us from the evil one.

For if you forgive other people when they sin against you,
your heavenly Father will also forgive you. But if you do
not forgive others their sins, your Father will not forgive
your sins."

Notice a few things:

First, prayer isn't for show. It's an inside world thing that can and should be outworked both when we're alone and with others. So we need to ask our motivation when praying. Am I trying to sound smart to impress people? Am I attempting to teach or control those listening? Am I filling God in on the details because I think He's far away and uninterested? Or am I simply longing to know God more?

Next, we're a part of a family, and prayer is a unity-bonding agent. Jesus' begins each line with a plural "our" and "us." So when we pray, it's way more than just about us. Prayer can realign our minds, wills, and emotions from being on ourselves and onto God and others too.

And lastly, because our heavenly Father already knows what's going on inside and around us, it can cause us to ask, "Why pray?". Ever felt that way?

It's important to catch that prayer is spending intentional time with Him, not simply educating him on what we need. God is not cold and formal, causing us to tiptoe into His presence. Instead, He's inviting us to come close into a welcoming and warm place where real life can happen, bringing all of who we really are to Him.

David reminds us in Psalm 62v8, *"Trust in him at all times, you people; pour out your hearts to him, for God is our refuge."*

Bible Project video to watch

- **Psalms** (thebibleproject.com/explore/psalms)

Bible Project Podcasts (optional)

- **Praying & Acting** (thebibleproject.com/podcast/ practicing-faith-part-3-praying-acting)
- **The Lord's Prayer** (thebibleproject.com/podcast/ matthew-p10-lords-prayer)

What does this mean for me today?

We pick up onto tons of wrongs ideas about God. It's just how it is. But as we looked at what prayer really is, we see it's the back and forth interaction with God, the very intention for the foundation of our lives. Today, may you know and enjoy the presence of God with you in your everyday moments. Spend time reading the Bible. It's where we learn the tone of God's voice. And as you read, talk with Him, listening for His whisper.

Something I learned in this chapter

A question raised in this chapter

9. The Church

The big idea

The church is a community of people rescued by faith from the power and effect of sin by the grace of Jesus Messiah, now set apart to love God and love people.

Verse to put to memory

"But you are a chosen people, a royal priesthood, a holy nation, God's special possession, that you may declare the praises of him who called you out of darkness into his wonderful light. Once you were not a people, but now you are the people of God; once you had not received mercy, but now you have received mercy." 1 Peter 2v9-12

The church is a God-filled community of people rescued by faith from the power and effect of sin by the grace of Messiah Jesus, now set apart to live enjoying and glorifying God. A unified community on a mission to the widow and orphan and foreigner, inviting all to a full and whole life found in Jesus. A community that celebrates and remembers the grace and kindness and truths of God through reading the Scriptures, song, baptism, and communion (each, a form of worship).

Biblically, we get the word *church* from *Ekklesia* (Greek: ἐκκλησίᾳ) meaning the assembly or community of the LORD. Church then is both universal (overall time, all over the world) and local (now and here).

Unity exists in the agreement that:

- The Scriptures are inspired by God.
- That Jesus was fully God in the flesh.
- That Jesus took our place of judgment for the wrong we've done (also called substitutionary atonement).
- The need to follow Jesus. Giving our allegiance to Him.
- The Spirit empowers the church.

- And the mission of the church to the world.

Local churches will put their time and energy toward different causes and have different leadership structures, and that's okay.

Here's an example.

Let's say one local church in the slums focuses on feeding the poor and have numerous small teams led by deacons.

Wonderful.

While another local church located in the Hollywood Hills may have a strong emphasis on teaching mission for the purpose of people putting their finances towards supporting the church in the slums.

Great.

Each church is on a mission to make God's glory visible, but how they make it happen is unique to their context and calling.

Life tip: As you grow up, move, and possibly change churches, be careful not to fall into the trap of comparing one church's value to another. While it's true some churches are heartier than others at certain times, the enemy loves to cause division as we compare *how and* *where* local churches decide to put their resources like time and money. Our job is to love God and people wherever we are.

Acts 2 is a key text in seeing the outworking of the church. We see the profession of faith in Jesus as God's **MESSIAH** and a call to turn around (repent) and be baptized, which led to more and more people saying *yes* to Jesus.

The church was growing and becoming influential. And even more, God was with and among the people in power. Wonders and signs yes, but also in the day-to-day care for those in need.

They celebrated the good news of Jesus' through communion, prayer, and shared the Gospel (**EVANGELISM**) with anyone who would listen. They also worshiped together through song (among other ways).

Worship is simply our *agreement response* to the goodness of God.

Bible Project Podcast (optional)

- **A Life of Learning** (thebibleproject.com/podcast/why-church-matters-part-1-life-learning)

What does this mean for me today?

Because we're not created or intended to do this on our own, who am I learning to enjoy and follow Jesus with? Who am I talking with about Jesus? Who am I wrestling through life stuff with? Who am I praying for on an ongoing basis, and who am I allowing to pray for me?

Find a few people and start talking openly about life and Jesus.

Something I learned in this chapter

A question raised in this chapter

10. The new heavens and the new earth

The big idea

"Heaven and earth were meant to overlap, and Jesus is on a mission to bring them together once and for all."
The Bible Project

Verse to put to memory

Then I saw "a new heaven and a new earth," for the first heaven and the first earth had passed away, and there was no longer any sea. I saw the Holy City, the new Jerusalem, coming down out of heaven from God, prepared as a bride beautifully dressed for her husband.

And I heard a loud voice from the throne saying, "Look! God's dwelling place is now among the people, and he will dwell with them. They will be his people, and God himself will be with them and be their God. 'He will wipe every tear from their eyes. There will be no more death' or mourning or crying or pain, for the old order of things has passed away."

He who was seated on the throne said, "I am making everything new!" Then he said, "Write this down, for these words are trustworthy and true."

Revelation 21v1-4

<u>Going deeper</u>

The story of the Bible begins in a garden. This garden was right and good. There were plants and trees. Food. Real organic fruit, aka sugar. Rivers, one of which Genesis says even had gold in it. Everything people needed to thrive.

Then it fell apart as people chose to sin by pulling away from God.

But as we read the story, we see God didn't give up on humanity or creation. In fact, in the book of Revelation, we see God recreating all things one day into a new kind of garden. One even more wonderful than the first. We call this new garden, *the new heavens and the new earth*.

It's a God-promise we can look forward to. The Bible word for this is *hope*.

Eschatology is "the study of the end." More specifically, it's the study of where things are going. In one sense, it's the actions of God toward His rescue plan to save humanity that came to fulfillment in Jesus.

As Jesus people, we study eschatology because it leads us to evangelism[52]. And because it leads to hope, faith, godliness, prayer, and worship as we recognize and embrace God is good, directing all things towards renewal.

If I were to ask you which book of the Bible comes to mind when thinking of what will happen in the future, what would you say?

Revelation?

I think most of us would go there. But there's something super important to catch here. Over the past few decades, a significant shift in focus has happened... and not for the best.

Although the central image of Revelation is the Lamb of God (Jesus), most of our time and energy and discussion has been spent talking about the details of our tomorrows.

95

"What's your view on the Tribulation? On the Millennium? How about the Rapture?"

Entire series of pop-culture books have been written, maybe with good intentions, but have unfortunately drawn our attention off of Jesus and onto unknowable future timing and outworking details that were never intended to be the point when it comes to eschatology (or the book of Revelation for that matter).

That said, here's a better way of thinking about the new heavens and new earth, eschatology, the letters in Revelation, and all that stuff.

Five ways Revelation is interpreted (each has minor differing views within them):

- A *preterist* reads Revelation and says the prophecies in chapters 4-19 have already happened – either during the fall of Jerusalem (70 AD) or during the fall of Rome in 476 AD.
- A *historicist* reads Revelation as a chronological history of events taking place beyond the first century – looking through history, placing the events on a calendar.
- A *futurist* reads the events in Revelation chapters 4-19 as yet to come, each taking place sometime in the future.
- An *idealist* reads Revelation not as actual events that have or will happen, but as symbols or timeless

truths.

- And finally, an *eclectic view* reads Revelation with a mix of the other four. An eclectic interpretation says it's important to read Revelation with a first-century mindset (preterist), that Revelation is true to history (historical), that Revelation looks forward (futurist), and that the symbols in Revelation do align with timeless truths (idealist).

So there you go. These five interpretations are responses to the bigger question in Revelation than those associated with a Tribulation, Millennium, or Rapture.

It's also important to note, within eschatology are **death** and **judgement**.

Physically, death is the separation between the material and immaterial. "Spiritually" death is the separation between God and humanity. But the good news is that within the Christian faith, death does not mean the end of existence. While everyone will physically die (unless Jesus returns first) because Jesus conquered death, there is life after death, eternal and forever-full life.

But because God is good and holy, judgment also exists. It's easy to become defensive, wanting to throw this reality away, but is that what you actually want? We're thankful that the person who harms us is judged fairly. We're thankful for systems that keep us safe as they judge right and wrong, yet we don't want the same rule applied to us. Even still, God is good and will judge each of us for how we choose to live and think and act. Yes, Jesus removes our sin, taking our judgment, but how we live matters. And because God is just, there will be judgement and rewards given to each person.

At this point, you may be wondering which view is correct. And while I lean towards one view myself, what's more important is recognizing there are details we don't need to figure out.

God gives us enough to know one thing for sure. He's good, and we can trust Him. And so when it comes to eschatology, we all agree on one thing. God is going show up in a new way, everyone will have to answer for the way they lived, and He'll make all things new that want to be made new.

Excellent job getting through all that! What's your big takeaway?

Bible Project videos to watch

- **Heaven & Earth** (thebibleproject.com/explore/heaven-earth)
- **Day of the Lord** (thebibleproject.com/explore/day-lord)

What does this mean for me today?

God's promise to remake the world leads us towards an ultimate hope that everything is going to be okay. And, because we're a part of God's family, He's tasked us to bring heaven-stuff into our spaces today.

So where can I bring hope, restoration, reconciliation, goodness, beauty, joy, etc. into those I'm with and around today?

Something I learned in this chapter

A question raised in this chapter

Going even deeper (totally optional)

While these next two sets of views certainly aren't the main point of this chapter, I do want you to be aware of them. Unfortunately, they seem to cause more arguments and disunity than almost anything else. I'd suggest sticking with our big idea.

God gives us enough to know one thing for sure. He's
good, and we can trust Him. And so when it comes to
eschatology, we all agree on one thing. God is going show
up in a new way, everyone will have to answer for the
way they lived, and He'll make all things new that want to
be made new.

Here we go...

Three ways the Millennium has been understood:

- A *premillennial* eschatology says Christ comes to start
  the Millennium, then after the Millennium, He judges
  everyone and sets up the new heavens and earth.
- A *postmillennial* eschatology says the Millennium
  begins because the Gospel wins, nations convert, then
  Christ comes after the Millennium to judge everyone
  and set up the new heavens and earth.
- An *amillennial* eschatology says there won't be a time
  of universal peace or righteousness (Millennium) on
  this earth (some say it will occur in the new heavens
  and new earth). Instead, Christ comes to judge
  everyone and set up the new heavens and earth.

Three ways the Tribulation of the church has been
understood:

- A pretribulational view says that when Jesus comes,
  He'll take the church with Him into heaven (God's
  space) during the Tribulation on earth. After that,

He'll bring the church back to earth for the Millennium, then the new heavens and new earth begin. This is often called a classic dispensational view.

- A postribulational view says that Jesus comes after the Tribulation, the church will meet Him in the air, but then joins Him into the Millennium and the new heavens and new earth.
- A midtribulational view says Jesus comes after the Tribulation, the church meets Him in the air (to avoid the wrath of God), but we join Him into the Millennium and the new heavens and new earth.

Can you guess what I'll say about these views? Yup, you're right. God is good, and we can trust Him. Avoid getting caught up in the details. Keep your eyes on Jesus.

11. Our life work

The big idea

As Jesus people, we step into the life work of remaining in Him. staying aware of His love for us and those around us. We're tasked with living lives of justice and righteousness, living right with people, ourselves, and God.

Verse to put to memory

"Therefore, if anyone is in Christ, the new creation has come: The old has gone, the new is here! All this is from God, who reconciled us to himself through Christ and gave us the ministry of reconciliation: that God was reconciling the world to himself in Christ, not counting people's sins against them. And he has committed to us

the message of reconciliation." 2 Corinthians 5v17-19

Going deeper

God and humanity and the Law and holiness and sin and the Gospel and a bunch of big theological terms that show God's love for us and baptism and communion and prayer and the Church and the new heavens and the new earth are all good to understand but pretty useless if they just sit in our brains.

As memorized truths and principles and rules and laws and concepts and ideas, they have no life in them. Can you imagine someone saying they're a professional basketball coach without ever stepping on a court or touching a ball? That'd be crazy. But the enemy loves to tell us that simply *knowing about* is the same as *really knowing*.

It's not.

The truth is, as we continue to choose to believe that Jesus is who He says He is, our new family identity is rich with purpose and work for us to do. Yup, God has work for you to do today, and it begins by aligning with His family values and ways.

Because Jesus is God, we live under His authority, knowing He is good! We step into

the life work of remaining in Him, staying aware of His love for us and those around us. We're tasked with living lives of justice and righteousness; living right with people, ourselves, and God.

Check out what 1 Peter 2v9-12 says, *"But you are a chosen people, a royal priesthood, a holy nation, God's special possession, that you may declare the praises of him who called you out of darkness into his wonderful light. Once you were not a people, but now you are the people of God; once you had not received mercy, but now you have received mercy."*

It outlines our identity as God's family, commissions us to worship God through song and truth statements, and reminds us of what God has done for us. But that's only the beginning, open your Bible and read the rest of the chapter.

No really, stop. Open your Bible and read 1 Peter 2.

...

As you read, did you notice it was super practical everyday stuff for the author's audience? It was relational stuff. It was intentional decision-making stuff and watching how we speak and act.

And this is our life work. To cultivate trust that God is for us, over us, with us, in us, and that our everyday moments are the fields we get to work in. "Resurrection life"[53] seems to sums it up well.

Sound like a big job? It is. And it's not at the same time. Jesus never gives us a task He doesn't equip us to complete. If He calls us to do something, we can count on Him being the One who will see us through. Engaging fully with the life work Jesus gives us requires all of ourselves. This is because the Gospel resurrects *every* part of us. "Will we allow it?" is the question.

I love what Paul says in 2 Corinthians 5v17-19, *"Therefore, if anyone is in Christ, the new creation has come: The old has gone, the new is here! All this is from God, who reconciled us to himself through Christ and gave us the ministry of reconciliation: that God was reconciling the world to himself in Christ, not counting people's sins against them. And he has committed to us the message of reconciliation."*

We've been set free, and now we get to live setting other people free. Free people, free people! If we've been totally and completely forgiven, then who are we to hold judgment against others? Jesus tells a sobering parable in Matthew 18v21-35 about this very thing. The next time you find yourself unwilling to forgive someone, read through the story and have a conversation with God. It won't be easy, and it may not lead you to forgive them anytime soon, but the perspective is sobering, the invitation unmistakable.

So our life work is both internal and external. Our life work requires us to bend both our thoughts and desires and ways of seeing people, and our actions and reactions, to His.

And the best part? We've been given everything we need! The Holy Spirit teaches and guides and reminds us when we're off the path, inviting us to return. God is the ultimate Spoiler Alerter. The Scriptures are filled with stories of people before us living every possible way, and we get to see their outcomes. God uses the Scriptures to shape our thinking to true reality. And so our final chapter will be all about the Bible.

Bible Project video to watch

- **Justice** (thebibleproject.com/explore/justice)

What does this mean for me today?

If Jesus has forgiven me, setting me free from the judgment I deserve, then I can no longer hold judgment against those around me. Who am I angry with that I need to forgive? Or who do I judge that I need let go of my ability to judge them?

Sometimes it's tough for me to find words in these

situations. Here's a prayer that may help get you started:

"Name, I unconditionally forgive you. Name, I release you from all my judgments and expectations. Name, I give up my right to judge you. Name, I bless you, and in Jesus, I love you."[54]

Something I learned in this chapter

A question raised in this chapter

12. The Bible

The big idea

The Bible is God's gift to us for learning what He's like and hearing His invitation to a free life. God uses the Scriptures to shape our thinking to true reality so that we can live this *Jesus resurrection life* here and now!

Verse to put to memory

"There's nothing like the written Word of God for showing you the way to salvation through faith in Christ Jesus. Every part of Scripture is God-breathed and useful one way or another—showing us truth, exposing our rebellion, correcting our mistakes, training us to live God's way. Through the Word we are put together and shaped up for the tasks God has for us." 2 Timothy 3v15b-17

We said in Part 1 that the Scriptures are historical documents recording the stories of real people and real places and real moments.

We said the Bible includes a handful of writing styles and types of literature, from narrative to poetry to songs to letters to bite-sized wisdom takeaways – using metaphors and countless literary devices.

And we said the Bible is a roadmap to where humanity has been, where we are today, and where we're headed tomorrow.

But we also said it's even more than that. It's where we learn what God is like and find His invitation to a free life. A full life. The life we're all longing for. The Bible calls it *eternal life*, and it started before we ever became aware.

God uses the Scriptures to shape our thinking to true reality so that we can live this *Jesus resurrection life* here and now.

Dallas Willards says it this way. "The Bible expresses the mind of God, since God himself speaks to us through its pages. Thus we, in understanding the Bible, come to share his thoughts. And attitudes and even come to share his life through his Word. Scripture is a communication that establishes communion and opens the way to union, all in a way that is perfectly understandable once we begin to have experience of it. We will be spiritually safe in our use of the Bible if we follow a simple rule: Read with a submissive attitude. Read with a readiness to surrender all you are – all your plans, opinions, possessions, positions."

So good.

Bible Project videos to watch

How to Read The Bible Series
(thebibleproject.com/explore/how-to-read-the-bible)

- What is the Bible? (5 min)
- Biblical Story (5 min)
- Literary Styles (5 min)
- Ancient Jewish Meditation Literature (4 min)
- Plot (5 min)
- Character (5 min)
- Setting (5 min)
- Design Patterns (6 min)
- The Gospel (5 min)
- Poetry (5 min)
- Metaphor in Biblical Poetry (5 min)
- The Book of Psalms (5 min)
- The Prophets (5 min)
- The Books of Solomon (5 min)
- The Law (6 min)

What does this mean for me today?

Reading and thinking about the words in the Bible is really important if we want to know God more. Sometimes we may feel like reading and other days we may not, so most of us can benefit from a tool that helps us form the pattern of reading the Bible each day.

Whether it's the One Year Bible, the Read Scripture app, or a Bible reading plan inside the YouVersion app if you're not already in the habit of opening up the Scriptures each day, today is a great day to start!

Something I learned in this chapter

A question raised in this chapter

Going even deeper (totally optional, but suggested)

I wrote a short chapter that will give you a bit more context and help with reading the Bible in my book, Moving from god to Abba. See chapter "Reading the Scriptures."

Part three: A few helpful words, ideas, and themes. Let's call it, "What's that mean?"

The **Apostles Creed** is a helpful statement produced no later than the fourth century summarizing the teachings of the apostles.

I believe in God, the Father almighty,
creator of heaven and earth.
I believe in Jesus Christ, his only Son, our Lord,
who was conceived by the Holy Spirit
and born of the virgin Mary.
He suffered under Pontius Pilate,
was crucified, died, and was buried;

he descended to hell.
The third day he rose again from the dead.
He ascended to heaven
and is seated at the right hand of God the Father
almighty.
From there he will come to judge the living and the dead.
I believe in the Holy Spirit,
the holy catholic* church,
the communion of saints,
the forgiveness of sins,
the resurrection of the body,
and the life everlasting. Amen.

Atonement: "All over the New Testament, we hear how the death of Jesus was an atonement for our sins, covering the debt that humans owe God for contributing to all the evil and death in the world. The New Testament also talks about the atonement of Jesus Christ as a purification. Like the blood of the animal sacrifices, it is now Christ's blood that washes away all of the damage and side-effects of sin, purifying and sanctifying the world." -The Bible Project

Attributes are caused by essence.

Belief systems range from a faith that no God or gods exist (such as Naturalism) to those which include millions of gods (such as Hinduism), while still others disregard the terms "God" or "gods" altogether and put their faith in there being a universal force or energy. Some of these faith systems say the Divine is knowable while others do not. Here are a few key terms when it comes to theological faith systems:

- A **universalist** says all paths lead to "God".
- A **deist** says there is a creator God, but that He's not active in creation.
- A **theist** says there is an active (personal: able to worship, pray to/with) creator God.
- A **polytheist** says there are many gods (one for health, one for crops, one for relationships, etc.)
- An **atheist** denies theism, saying there is no God.
- An **agnostic** says there's no way to know if God exists.
- A **gnostic** says there's a force or energy that can be tapped into.
- A **dualist** says there are two gods locked in cosmic battle, that one is good and the other is evil.
- A **pantheist** says everything is God.
- A **monotheist** says there is one personal and knowable God.
- A **trinitarian monotheist** says there is one personal and knowable God that has revealed Himself as one in essence and three in person.

Blessing is adoration or deep love. See chapter "What Happened?" in my book, Moving from god to Abba for more on this.

Character is what we know of someone or something based on their/its attributes.

Christ means *God's anointed One*, or the Savior. Jesus fulfilled this Messianic role. When you read *Jesus Christ*, you can rightly say *Jesus Messiah*, or *Jesus the anointed promised One by God* – that's kinda long though :)

Christian means "little Christ" or one who imitates the Christ.

Conversion is faith/trust and repentance. It's trusting that God is truth, right, good and that His way is the way, which then leads to a changing of our mind about values.

Essence is the intrinsic nature or indispensable quality of something.

Evangelism means to share the good news of Jesus' death, burial, and resurrection through words and actions.

To glorify God means to make Him a big deal.

Justice and righteousness is the way God told Abram to live in Genesis 18v19. It's the foundation of what it looks like to live a part of God's family and results in peace and joy (Romans 14v17). Justice is living right with people. Righteousness is living right with yourself and God.

Justification is God saying someone, like me and you, is not guilty (forgiveness), and even more is righteous (acceptance). It's external in that God speaks it over us, a one time moment. It's God's work for us, a new identity, by grace as we believe (faith).

Messiah was the historic term used by the prophets to point forward to the day when God would make a way for humanity to be made right with God. Jesus fulfilled this role.

Non-dualism is seeing all of life as connected, valuable, and in God. Both the seen and unseen, one. Dualism says there is a spiritual life and a tangible life (as one example). Jesus used everyday objects in His parables about what the Kingdom of God is like to help us recognize all of *life is spiritual*.

Reconciliation is the result of Jesus' taking our place of judgment because of our sin. It's the ending of us being estranged from God.

Repent means to turn around and change your thinking. It's the process of recognizing and owning that we're wrong, that we're heading away from God, then turning around; face to face again. Thank God He's patient with us, forgiving and welcoming us home – every time. My favorite story of repentance is one Jesus told in Luke 15v11-32. When you read it, notice what happens in the son's soul (mind, will, and emotions) and in his physicality.

Resurrection is coming back to life after dying.

Apparently, the test in Hebrew culture for being dead-dead meant you were dead on the third day. It's no coincidence Jesus came back on the third day :)

Righteous means you're right with God. Pure gift.

Salvation means conversion, God's saving work, which began before the fall in Genesis 3 as God offered the covenant for humanity to "be saved" through Messiah Jesus.

Sanctification[55] is the ongoing process of becoming more holy by the power of Holy Spirit in us. It's internal in that our lives are being formed more into the ones God says we are as we allow God's words to change and shape and lead the way we think, aligning our of thinking and living with God's way. It's the working out of our salvation because God is working in me by His power. Again, it's God's work for us by grace as we believe (faith).

"The Scriptures" and "The Bible" are often used interchangeably.

Sin is a departure from God's standards of uprightness. It begins with saying *no* to God, violating what He says is good and right and true and just.

Substitutionary atonement is Jesus taking our place for the debt our sin requires (death). The Old Testament image is of a perfect lamb fulfilling a needed sacrifice.

The great Shema was a super important prayer for the Israelite people, God's people. It re-centered their soul (mind, will, and emotions) back onto God when everything around them screamed for their attention. Check out the Bible Project video called "What is the Shema?"

A **theologian** is someone whose life work is studying and explaining what we know of God.

Theology is the study of God.

YHWH is the Hebrew way of referring to the creator God. In the Bible, you'll see it written as LORD in all caps.

About the Author

Hey, I'm nate. A pastor and graphic designer living and working in Portland, Oregon.

My goal is simple. To show, tell, and express the wonder and goodness of the Father, Son, and Holy Spirit in ways you can embrace both individually and communally.

Instagram: @natekupish
Email: hello@natekupish.com

Other writings: natekupish.com

Endnotes

[1] As of November 2019. Keep checking their site for fun new content.

[2] Romans 14v17

[3] See Exodus 34

[4] Romans 8v14-16

[5] Before this, the term "Godhead" was used to express the same reality.

[6] "...third century Latin theologian Tertulian as a way of drawing together the emerging Christian doctrine of God. The word consists of two elements, *tri and unity*, and each of these elements is crucial to an adequate understanding of the doctrine." p101, The Mystery of God, written by Stephen Boyer and Christopher Hall

[7] Reeves, Michael. The Good God. Paternoster, 2012. pp.x

[8] Boyer, Steven D., and Christopher A. Hall. "The Mystery of the Trinity." The Mystery of God: Theology for Knowing the Unknowable. Grand Rapids, MI: Baker Academic, 2012. 19. Print.

[9] Boyer, Steven D., and Christopher A. Hall. "The Mystery of the Trinity." *The Mystery of God: Theology for Knowing the Unknowable*. Grand Rapids, MI: Baker Academic, 2012. 45. Print. Referring to, Early Christian Prayers, ed. A Hamman, trans. Walter Mitchell (London: Longmans Green, 1961), 162.

[10] Boyer, Steven D., and Christopher A. Hall. "The Mystery of the Trinity." The Mystery of God: Theology for Knowing the Unknowable. Grand Rapids, MI: Baker Academic, 2012. 102-05. Print.

[11] A few examples: The Father as creator, designer, and planner as seen in Ephesians 1v3-6 and 1 Peter 1v2. The Son as the life giver and redeemer as seen in 1 Corinthians 8v8, John 1v3, and Ephesians 1v3-15. And the Holy Spirit as the One who convicts and teaches as in John 16v8-11, 1 Corinthians 2v13. Yet, texts like Acts 17v24, 1 Corinthians 8v6, John 1v2, Genesis 1v2, and Psalm 90v2 seem to say that *they* (depending on the text; the Father and Son or all *three*) are one, that they act together.

[12] Including acts or actions.

[13] The character of God.

[14] Because God is relationship within Himself, the uniqueness of Divine Relationship is that He reveals Himself *in order to* draw people into relationship with Him.

[15] First in recognizing, then in receiving, intimate relationship with God.

[16] Based on the Scripture narrative, sin has broken our knowing of God (soteriologically), therefore His divine revelation to us of Himself is necessary for relationship.

[17] The following are some means of special revelation, not an exhaustive list.

[18] From what? Read Romans 1v18-32.

[19] Matthew 11v27

[20] See Exodus 3v6 and Matthew 22v32

[21] Hebrews 13v8

[22] Gerry Breshears "Spirit Outline".

[23] The quoted summary sentences for each communicable and incommunicable attribute of God are from: Grudem, Wayne A., and K. Erik. Thoennes. "The Character of God: "Incommunicable" Attributes. How is God different from us?" Systematic Theology, Zondervan, 2008, p. 156-168

[24] Job 36v26, Isaiah 40v28, Revelation 1v8, Hebrews 13v8.

[25] Psalm 102v25-27, Malachi 3v6, James 1v17, Psalm 33v11.

[26] Acts 17v24-25, Job 41v11, Psalm 50v10-12, John 17v5, John 17v24, Revelation 4v11, John 1v3, Romans 11v35-36, 1 Corinthians 8v6, Psalm 90v2, Exodus 3v14, Isaiah 43v7, Ephesians 1v11-12, Revelation 4v11, Isaiah 62v3-5, Zephaniah 3v17-18.

[27] Books to consider on this topic:

- Christopher Hall and Steven Boyer, The Mystery of God: Theology for Knowing the Unknowable
- Douglas Moo, Romans: The NIV Application Commentary
- A.W. Tozer, The Knowledge of the Holy
- Michael Reeves, The Good God
- Fred Sanders and Klaus Issler, Jesus in Trinitarian Perspective: An Intermediate Christology

[28] Richard Rohr. The Divine Dance: Exploring the Mystery of Trinity. 2004. MP3. *Please note, Rohr's perspective's are different than an Evangelical one in some areas of theology.*

[29] A phrase (or variation) used at least 90 times in the Scriptures.

[30] A Long Obedience in the Same Direction: Discipleship in an Instant Society, by Eugene H. Peterson, InterVarsity Press, 2019. p47

[31] Each quoted law below is from the Message Translation.

[32] Romans 5v10

[33] Romans 5v10

[34] Quote from The Bible Project: thebibleproject.com/explore/sacrifice-atonement/

[35] A few helpful verses on sanctification are Romans chapters 6 and 8, Titus 3v5, 1 Thessalonians 4v3 and 5v23, Hebrews 12v14, 2 Peter 3v18, and Jude 1v20.

[36] Revelation 13v8

[37] As seen in Ephesians 2v1-3 (for example)

[38] Romans 8

[39] Titus 3v5

[40] 1 Corinthians 1v18, Philippians 2v12, 2 Corinthians 2v15

[41] Romans 5v9, Romans 13v11

[42] Romans 12-16

[43] Examples include Arminian, Wesleyan, and Calvinistic.

[44] 2 Samuel 9, Romans 3-6 (3v24 and 4v4) Romans 11v5-6, Galatians 2-3, Galatians 5v1, 13; Ephesians 2v1-10, Philippians 1v6, 2 Timothy 1v9, Acts 15v11, Hebrews 13v9

[45] Acts 4v33, 1 Corinthians 15v10, 2 Corinthians 9v8, 14 and 12v9, Ephesians 4v7, 2 Timothy 2v1

[46] Romans 6v1, 14-17, 2 Corinthians 6v1ff; 8v1-7; Ephesians 1v7, 2v5-8

[47] Acts 11v21, 14v15, 26:18; Acts 3v19, 20v21, 26v20; 1 Thessalonians 1v9; James 5v20, 2 Peter 3v9

[48] Romans 1v16-17, 3v21-31, 4v1-5v1, 9v30-32; Galatians 2v14-3v3, Acts 13v38-39, James 2v14-21, Colossians 1v23, Hebrews 3v14

[49] John 3v3-8, Ezekiel 36v25-28, John 1v13, 1 Peter 1v23, Hebrews 10v15-22, Titus 3v3-7

[50] Dedicated to God for service as in 1 Corinthians 1v30, Hebrews 10v10, 14, Ephesians 1v1, 1 Corinthians 1v2, 6v11 and ongoing ethical and moral conforming to Christ as in 2 Corinthians 7v1, Hebrews 12v10, 14; Ephesians 1v4, Romans 6v22

[51] John 6v39-40, Romans 8v29, 1 Corinthians 15v12-58, Philippians 3v20-21, 1 John 3v2

[52] Ultimately because we know we'll all stand before God for judgment.

[53] Got this phrase from Eugene Peterson's, Practice Resurrection: A Conversation on Growing Up in Christ, who got the phrase from environmental activist and poet Wendell Berry. This is a great read on what it means to grow in living Jesus' way.

[54] SOZO prayer of forgiveness.

[55] Romans 6, 8. Titus 3v5. 1 Thessalonians 4v3, 5v23. Hebrews 12v14. 2 Peter 3v18. Jude 1v20.

Made in the USA
Middletown, DE
06 January 2020